AN ORDINARY DAY WITH JESUS

WITH JESUS

Experiencing the Reality of God in Your Everyday Life

AN ORDINARY DAY WITH JESUS

Experiencing the Reality of God in Your Everyday Life

Participant's Guide

John Ortberg and Ruth Haley Barton

WILLOW
Willow Creek Resources

ZONDERVAN™

GRAND RAPIDS, MICHIGAN 49530 USA

13 /DC/ 27 26 25 24

Dedication

Dallas Willard has been a teacher, mentor, and friend to many people—including the authors of this course—who seek to follow the way of Christ. The whole idea of building a course around spending the day with Jesus came from Dallas' teaching and we use it with his characteristic gracious permission.

With deep appreciation and much love, *An Ordinary Day with Jesus* is dedicated to Dallas Willard. "The . . . secret of the ordinary is that it is made to be a receptacle of the divine, a place where the life of God flows."*

* Dallas Willard, *The Divine Conspiracy.*

Contents

Preface

What does it take to make a day great? Often we think it takes some piece of extra-ordinary news—winning the lottery, getting a huge promotion, driving home during rush hour and not hitting any traffic jams.

But the truth is, any ordinary day can become extra-ordinarily great by doing one simple thing—spending it with God.

Too often people spend months or years or even decades feeling guilty about how they're approaching their spiritual lives. But this is not God's will for any of his children. He has another plan. His great desire is to walk together with each child of his through the ordinary days of their lives.

And this is his plan for you as well. You can do this. God would not have commanded it if it were not so.

You have a great privilege—to learn about and experience life with God:
   how to begin and end your days with God
   how to give your everyday relationships to him, and to be alone with
      him in a way that feeds your soul
   how to actually work with him right alongside you
   how to listen to the Holy Spirit
   how to identify the spiritual pathways that can aid you in
      experiencing ongoing connection with God
   how to reflect on the pace of your life and hear God address you
      through Scripture
   how to plan for and commit to spending an entire day with Jesus

But the greatest learning will happen outside this course. It will emerge in the minutes and hours of daily living. Every moment is an opportunity to say, "Here's my chance to learn from Jesus. He's right here, right now, ready to live in magnificent partnership with me."

Here's your chance.

Acknowledgments

There is nothing more exciting than a church full of people who are experiencing the reality of God in the midst of the ordinary. And so it is with deepest gratitude that we acknowledge the community of faith in which we have learned and practiced the truths presented in this course.

To the elders and the congregation at Willow Creek Community Church for providing the context for the creation of this course. Hundreds of people made themselves available as "guinea pigs" to experience the course in various phases of its development and to provide us with thoughtful and valuable feedback.

To Bill Hybels for providing guidance during the initial phases of shaping the content.

To Jim Mellado, Joe Sherman, and Christine Anderson of the Willow Creek Association for believing in this project and coming alongside us with the resources and expertise needed to publish this course. Christine has shepherded, managed, and prodded this project with skill, persistence, and love. It would not have come to fruition without her.

To Wendy Seidman and Sue Drake for contributing the instructional design expertise that neither one of us has!

To Judson Poling for going beyond the call of duty in capturing this course in written form throughout *multiple* iterations and revisions. His mind and soul are part of each session.

To Steve Pederson, Mark Demel, Scott Dyer, and the staff of IMS Productions for their expertise and enthusiasm in working with us to create video segments that touch the heart.

To our volunteer team, including Keri Kent, Jim Pio, Dalene Strieff, Bill Hayes, Diana Searls, Art Holton, and Linda Bryant. We are grateful for their prayers and support as we developed the content and ministry of this course within the walls of Willow Creek.

To Jodi Walle, Karen Dickson, and Tiffany Staman for their patient administrative support throughout the various developmental phases of this project.

And to our families: John—Nancy, Laura, Mallory, and Johnny; Ruth—Chris, Charity, Bethany, and Haley. Thank you for bearing with the sacrifices of time necessary to carry out this project and, most of all, for providing us with ordinary moments made extraordinary by your love and presence in our lives.

LIVING IN

1
Monday

JESUS'
NAME

LIVING IN JESUS' NAME

Something Missing

Notes:

Every Ordinary Day in Jesus' Name

The Apostle Paul believed the place to grow close to God is precisely in our _____*everyday*_____ lives.

> *Whatever you do, whether in word or deed,*
> *do it all in the name of the Lord Jesus,*
> *giving thanks to God the Father through him.*
> (Colossians 3:17)

> *I am with you always ...*
> (Matthew 28:20)

The heart of spiritual life is to do everything *with* Jesus, *in* his name—the way he would do it in our place, knowing he *is* actually present.

What Living in Jesus' Name Might Look Like in Your Life

- *Waking up*

- *Eating breakfast*

- *Driving*

- *Working*

- *Watching TV*

- *Worrying*

- *Doing ordinary household tasks*

- *Shopping*

- *Doing everyday relationships*

LIVING IN JESUS' NAME

One Day at a Time

We can only live in Jesus' name one day at a time.

> *Do not worry about tomorrow,*
> *for tomorrow will worry about itself.*
> *Each day has enough trouble of its own.*
> (Matthew 6:34)

> *This is the day the LORD has made;*
> *let us rejoice and be glad in it.*
> (Psalm 118:24)

If I am going to learn to spend an ordinary day with Jesus, it will have to be _this_ day.

It doesn't mean doing new things.

It means doing things you're ___already___ doing, but in new ways—
in Jesus' name.

SMALL GROUP ACTIVITY

Challenges to Doing Life in Jesus' Name

Ground rules for discussions:

Π No pressure

Π No advice

Π No faking

Directions:

1. Introduce yourself to the people at your table.

2. Share one or two of the activities listed below that are the hardest for you to do in Jesus' name, and explain why.

☐ *Sleeping*	☐ *Handling conflict*
☐ *Waking up*	☐ *Spending money*
☐ *Eating*	☐ *Driving*
☐ *Doing everyday relationships* (kids, spouse, neighbor, etc.)	☐ *Doing household chores*
	☐ *Watching TV*
☐ *Working*	☐ *Recreational activities*

LIVING IN JESUS' NAME

Beginning the Day with Jesus.

According to the Old Testament, the day begins _with him_ .

At night

> *There was evening, and there was morning—the first day.*
>
> (Genesis 1:5)

> Thinking about night as the beginning of the day reminds us that everything doesn't depend on us. We go to sleep, but God is working all through the night. So we don't have to be anxious or rushed. When we wake up, we will simply join him in his work.
>
> Eugene H. Peterson

Sleep

Sleep is an act of _trust_.

> *I lie down and sleep; I wake again,*
> *because the LORD sustains me.*
> (Psalm 3:5)

Sleep is a gift from God.

> *In vain you rise early and stay up late,*
> *toiling for food to eat—for*
> *he grants sleep to those he loves.*
> (Psalm 127:2)

LIVING IN JESUS' NAME

Get enough sleep.

_____Fatigue_____ is one of the greatest barriers to prayer and spiritual growth.

Resolve conflicts before going to bed.

> *It is a decisive rule of every Christian fellowship that every dissension that the day has brought must be healed in the evening.*
> *It is perilous for the Christian to lie down to sleep with an unreconciled heart.*
>
> Dietrich Bonhoeffer

> *Do not let the sun go down while you are still angry, and do not give the devil a foothold.*
>
> (Ephesians 4:26–27)

Invite Jesus to be with you when you wake.

Pray a simple prayer: "God, when I wake up, I want my first thoughts to be about you."

> *Great is his faithfulness; his mercies begin afresh each day.*
>
> (Lamentations 3:23, NLT)

SESSION ONE

Waking Up

ask Jesus to be with us for the day.

Renew your ___invitation___ to Jesus.

Speak to Jesus about any anxieties or concerns you feel.

> *For Christians, the beginning of the day should not be burdened and haunted by the various kinds of concerns that they face during the day. The Lord stands above the new day, for God has made it. All restlessness, all impurity, all worry and anxiety flee before him. Therefore, in the early morning hours of the day, may our many thoughts and our many idle words be silent and may the first word and the first thought belong to the one to whom our whole life belongs.*
>
> Dietrich Bonhoeffer

> *Cast all your anxiety on him because he cares for you.*
> (1 Peter 5:7)

Acknowledge your ___dependance___ on Jesus.

> *Come to me, all you who are weary and burdened, and I will give you rest.*
> (Matthew 11:28)

LIVING IN JESUS' NAME

Learning to Find God in Each Moment of the Day

We need to develop the skill of identifying God's presence in our lives.

Review the day with God.

INDIVIDUAL ACTIVITY

Review the Day with God

1. Be still for a moment, and quiet your mind.

2. Acknowledge that Jesus is present. Invite him to guide you.

3. Recall the beginning of the day when you first woke up. Watch that scene, as if on video. What is your reaction to what you see? Talk to God about that.

4. Continue through the video of your day, going from scene to scene. As you reflect on each one, some scenes may fill you with gratitude, others with regret. Speak directly to God about this. You may also want to pray for some of the people you interacted with during the day.

5. End your review with a prayer of thanksgiving for God's mercy and love. Ask him to refresh you as you sleep.

LIVING IN JESUS' NAME

Reviewing Your Day with God Regularly

Two things will begin to happen.

- You will become aware of recurring negative patterns. This will:
  —cause you to grow tired of your regrets
  —increase your desire to grow and change

- You will begin to be awed by God's presence in the ordinary moments of your life.

Course Overview

Session 2:   Everyday Relationships

Session 3:   Work

Session 4:   Leadings

Session 5:   Solitúde

Session 6:   Spiritual Pathways

Session 7:   Pace of Life.

Session 8:   Making the Ordinary Extraordinary

Course goal—to help you spend an ordinary day with Jesus.

It *is possible* to live *every day* with Jesus—one day at a time.

LIVING IN JESUS' NAME

SESSION**TWO**

EVERYDAY

RELATIONSHIPS

RELATIONSHIPS

Spiritual Gauges

The Wrong Gauge

___Boundary markers___ are external, superficial signs or practices that set one group apart from another.

For scribes and Pharisees: observing strict dietary laws, rigidly keeping the Sabbath, and circumcision.

> *Spirituality wrongly understood or pursued is a major source of human misery and rebellion against God.*
>
> Dallas Willard

SMALL GROUP ACTIVITY

Spiritual Gauges

1. Get in a group with two other people.

2. Answer the following questions:

- What are some wrong ways people in our day gauge spiritual health and maturity?

  - judge people by how they look then their
    - church attendance (from heart,
      weren reasons)
    - should not consentrate on "order service)
  - not as open to changes in service)
- some hymns no melody

- Do you sometimes use wrong spiritual gauges? What are they?

EVERYDAY RELATIONSHIPS

The Right Gauge

> *Teacher, which is the greatest commandment of the Law?*
> *Jesus replied, "Love the Lord your God with all your heart*
> *and with all your soul and with all your mind."*
> *This is the first and greatest commandment.*
> *And the second is like it: "Love your neighbor as yourself."*
> *All the Law and the Prophets*
> *hang on these two commandments.*
> (Matthew 22:36–40)

The right gauge is ___Love___.

Love for God & neighbors

> *If I have not love—even if I am knowledgeable,*
> *even if I do miracles, or give myself up as a martyr—*
> *I am nothing.*
> (1 Corinthians 13:1-3, paraphrased)

God is not interested in some abstract thing called your *spiritual* life.

God is interested in your ___life (all of it)___.

He wants you to be filled with love—love for him, and love for people.

VIDEO

Flying Lesson

Notes:

INDIVIDUAL ACTIVITY

Reflection on Flying Lesson

Use the space below to write your answers to the following questions:

1. Think about the two men on the plane and their contrasting reactions to the young woman. How are you like the irritated passenger? How are you like the compassionate passenger? What does this reveal about the gauge of love in your life?

    Easy to not be loving when tired
    or worried about self.
    ~~Need to see God in others~~
    Need to love others as God/Jesus
    have requested.

2. What barriers keep you from being a more loving person?

    Sin

    ask God to help us.

EVERYDAY RELATIONSHIPS

Using the Right Gauge: Training vs. Trying

> *Do you not know that in a race all the runners run,*
> *but only one gets the prize? Run in such a way as to get the prize.*
> *Everyone who competes in the games goes into strict training.*
> *They do it to get a crown that will not last;*
> *but we do it to get a crown that will last forever.*
> (1 Corinthians 9:24-25)

Definition of Training:

To train means to ___arrange___ my life around activities I can do that will enable me, over time, to do what I cannot do by direct effort alone.—Dallas Willard

exercise daily
Praying + reading God's word.

> *Train yourself to be godly.*
> (1 Timothy 4:7)

> *Everyone who is fully trained will be like [their] teacher.*
> (Luke 6:40)

Training is an indispensable ingredient for pursuing spiritual transformation.

We will have to train to be loving.

The purpose of such activities is not to demonstrate how spiritual we are.

Training activities exist to help us grow in love for God and other people and to become more like Christ.

Read God's word

ask God to help us love others especially ones hard to love.

RELATIONSHIPS

Three Ways to Train to Be More Loving

Jesus listened & asked questions.

What would Jesus do.

1. ☑ Listen.

brace

> *Everyone should be quick to listen,*
> *slow to speak and slow to become angry.*
>
> *(James 1:19)*

Use the phrase "Tell me ___more___."

Repeat what they saied to eet them know You are listening

2. ☑ Use touch.

UCLA study: We need at least eight to ten meaningful touches a day for our emotional health.

3. ☑ Speak words of love.

See Page 114 Dealing w/ conflicts

> Jesus, the Word who became flesh,
> was *"full of grace and … truth."*
>
> *(John 1:14)*

Words of grace	Words of truth
Comfort	Forgiveness
Encouragement	Reconciliation
Care and concern	Addressing conflict

Summary

— Love God & Love Others
   most important thing.

We Love others by listening
   to them.

   See page 114 - Dealing
                  w/ Conflict.

EVERYDAY RELATIONSHIPS

SESSION THREE

WORK

WORK

VIDEO

Work

Notes:

Job satisfaction

Why Work?

We work because we are made in the image of God.

> *My Father is always at his work to this very day,*
> *and I, too, am working.*
> (John 5:17)

Work is:

—not a curse but a blessing.

—partnering with God to care for his creation and serve others.

The most important thing you bring home from your work is ~~blessing~~ *you*.

Beginning Your Workday

Showing up on time

Greeting your coworkers or your children differently

Pray

—Tell God about your attitudes or feelings.

—Ask God to make you effective and successful.

—Ask God to partner with you throughout the day.

SMALL GROUP ACTIVITY

Beginning My Workday

1. Form a group with two other people.

2. Describe the beginning of your workday.

3. Share how you think it might be different if you were to begin your workday in Jesus' name.

WORK

During Your Workday

Setting

Place _____*symbols*_____ or reminders in your work setting.

A single word on a piece of paper (*peace, wisdom, serve*)

A favorite Scripture verse

> *Whatever you do, work at it with all your heart,
> as working for the Lord.*
> (Colossians 3:23)

Make sure your work setting is well ordered.

People

Look for opportunities to do simple acts of ___~~Be~~ *service*___.
          help   *Kindness*
"How may I serve you today?"

Learn from difficult people.

They help us grow in our ability to love.

They represent a learning opportunity.

Say to yourself, "School is in session; here's my chance to learn about love."

Receive Feedback Well

> ### Think of yourself with *"sober judgment."*
> (Romans 12:3)

Set aside your fears long enough to really hear what's being said.

Have a greater level of humility and openness.

Pray this prayer: "What is the truth I need to learn from this, Lord?"

Your work can become the center of your spiritual life.

Take Mini-Breaks

The Bible describes creation occurring with a daily rhythm:

Breaks in between

A day off at the end of every six

It is not more spiritual to work nonstop to exhaustion.

Take a short walk.

Make a brief phone call to a friend.

Take at least one day off out of every seven.

WORK

Two or three times a day, take five to ten minutes to stop your work, be quiet, and ___*focus*___ on God.

Thank him for his care for you.

Ask him for help.

We don't want to just work *for* God; we want to work *with* him.

Ending Your Workday

End each workday by taking a few moments to reflect on what you have done, and declare it ___*good*___.

End your day honestly.

Ask God for his help to work diligently the next day.

Pray and ask God for his strength to:

—be able to leave work behind

—enter fully into home life

End your workday in Jesus' name.

Two Additional Observations about Work

1. Unpaid Work

Your work, too, matters to God.

Money is *not* the measure of the value of your work in God's eyes.

2. Wrong Fit

God wants you to use your skills and giftedness in your work.

> *It is* wrong, *it is* sin, *to accept or remain in a position that you know is a mismatch for you. Perhaps that's a form of sin you've never even considered—the sin of staying in the wrong job. But God did not place you on this earth to waste away your years in labor that does not employ his design or purpose for your life, no matter how much you may be getting paid for it.*
>
> Arthur Miller

Give yourself to your current work as diligently as you can.

At the same time, explore other job opportunities.

WORK

The Ultimate Performance Review

Give yourself a performance review from God's perspective. Write your responses to the following questions.

What would God say about my approach to my daily work?

make to do list
Go to God in prayer

How is work affecting my heart?

Do work in service to God.

What would God affirm about my attitudes and habits?

will be positive

Where in my workday am I having the hardest time connecting with God?

when become negative

How might one ordinary day at work be different if I did it in partnership with God?

Would get all to do items done
and have joy in heart.
Declare it to be good.

SMALL GROUP ACTIVITY

The Ultimate Performance Review
(continued)

1. Form a group with two other people.

2. Discuss answers to the last question on the performance review: How might one ordinary day at work be different if I did it in partnership with God?

WORK

Summary

We work because we are made in the image of God.

We can experience God's presence with us at work by:

> Beginning and ending the workday in Jesus' name
>
> Paying attention to our work setting
>
> Paying attention to the people we work with
>
> Taking mini-breaks
>
> Taking at least one day off

God invites us to join him in his work as we do our work.

SESSION **FOUR**

LEADINGS

LEADINGS

Learning to Listen to God's Voice *speaking to us.*

We need to learn to:

Hear his voice

Filter out the noise of the world

I King 19: 11-13

How God Speaks

How human communication works:

When one person speaks, the listener is prompted to have new thoughts.

You allow the speaker to influence your thoughts.

Communication is simply ___*guiding*___ someone's thoughts with their cooperation.

People can guide your thoughts only indirectly, through physical means like sounds or sights.

God can guide your thoughts by speaking directly to your heart and mind.

> *A shepherd enters through the gate.*
> *The gatekeeper opens the gate for him, and the sheep hear his*
> *voice and come to him. He calls his own sheep by name*
> *and leads them out. After he has gathered his own flock,*
> *he walks ahead of them, and they follow him*
> *because they recognize his voice.*
>
> (John 10:2–4, NLT)

Jesus is our shepherd:

We need to recognize his voice so we can follow where he leads.

VIDEO

Leadings

Notes:

LEADINGS

SMALL GROUP ACTIVITY

Experiences with Leadings

1. Form a group with two other people.

2. Discuss the following questions:

   Have you ever had a prompting or leading?

   If so, how did you respond? What was the outcome?

   If not, how do you imagine you'd respond if such a leading did occur?

Three Key Learnings about Leadings

1. Hearing God's voice is learned behavior.

   The Bible teaches:

   Normal, psychologically healthy people *do* hear from God.

   It takes some time and _____Training_____ to learn how to hear God's voice.

> Then the Lord called Samuel. Samuel answered,
> "Here I am." And he ran to Eli and said, "Here I am; you called me."
> But Eli said, "I did not call; go back and lie down."
> So he went and lay down. Again the Lord called,
> "Samuel!" And Samuel got up and went to Eli and said,
> "Here I am; you called me." "My son," Eli said, "I did not call;
> go back and lie down." Now Samuel did not yet know the Lord.
> The word of the Lord had not yet been revealed to him.
> The Lord called Samuel a third time. And then Eli realized
> the Lord was calling the boy. So Eli told Samuel,
> "Go and lie down, and if he calls you, say,
> 'Speak, Lord, for your servant is listening.'"
>
> (1 Samuel 3:4–10)

Holy Spirit leads us.

A personal relationship with God is at the heart of Christianity, so _____Communicating_____ with him—and he with us—is at the heart of the relationship.

LEADINGS

We can invite God to teach us with the prayer: "Speak, Lord, for your servant is listening."

Number 22 - 21-31

2. God can speak to anyone.

He does not restrict his voice to Christian leaders or spiritual superstars.

3. God's voice has distinguishing characteristics.

   • He will always speak in ways consistent with his character.

   If you have anxious thought—it's not from God.

   We come to recognize God's promptings by:

   —Focusing on God's attributes

   —Learning from our personal experience

   —Studying his voice in Scripture

   We can learn to recognize God's voice from the way it affects our hearts.

   • Will always be consistent with _character / scripture._
   God is good. He brings peace
   • Will be consistent with who he made you to be. *(gifts from God)*

   • Will be consistent with love.

   A simple question to ask: Is this action selfish or loving?

Luke 24: 13-32

Must be still to hear God's voice / Holy Spirit.

VIDEO

Competing Voices

Notes:

"The Whisper Test"

Reflect on these questions

Summary

1) What do need to hear from God right now.

2) I will listen and be fully responsive.

SESSION **FIVE**

SOLITUDE

SOLITUDE

Solitude

Solitude is:

A time when we withdraw from the company of others in order to give God our undivided attention.

—Shut out external stimulation

—Allow ourselves to become quiet

Quiet Time

Notes: No distractions

Solitude is an __opportunity__ , not an obligation.

We need to plan how we spend our time with God. For example:

   silent listening

   Scripture reflection

   prayer

   journaling

   a slow meditative walk

   worship music

   singing praises

A plan helps us to stay focused.

Reading Scripture
Praying
Singing praises

SOLITUDE

Experiencing Solitude

1. Find a quiet place that is free of distractions.

Read p. 121

> *Very early in the morning, while it was still dark,*
> *Jesus got up, left the house and went off to a solitary place,*
> *where he prayed.*
>
> (Mark 1:35)

> *Then, because so many people were coming and going*
> *that they did not even have a chance to eat, [Jesus] said to*
> *[his disciples], "Come with me by yourselves to a quiet place*
> *and get some rest." So they went away by themselves*
> *in a boat to a solitary place.*
>
> (Mark 6:31-32)

The locations Jesus chose were _____solitary_____ and quiet.

We need to pay attention to *where* we meet with God.

Quiet + free of distraction.

2. _____Quiet_____ yourself in God's presence.

Breathe deeply

Slow down

3. Tell God what you need.   *Talk to God about everything.*

   Use a simple prayer:

   "God, I just want to be with you."

   "God, I need your guidance."

   "Lord, I want to feel your love."

   Be clear about what you would like to receive from God.

4. Use ___*Scripture*___ to listen to God.

   Read it slowly and deliberately.

   Notice the words or phrases that stand out and speak to your heart.

   What thoughts or emotions do you experience?

5. Be fully present.

   Give him your undivided attention.

   Speak to him directly about whatever you are thinking or feeling.

   Wandering thoughts:

   Aren't always a barrier to prayer

   May be a guide for prayer

SOLITUDE

6. Respond to what you hear God saying to you through Scripture or in prayer.

   Respond verbally or by writing in a journal.

   Start with: "God, what I hear you saying to me is ...."

7. Express gratitude and commitment.

INDIVIDUAL ACTIVITY

Experiencing Solitude

1. Find a quiet place that is free of distractions.

2. Quiet yourself in God's presence.
   - Begin by breathing deeply.
   - Slow down.
   - Become aware of God's presence with you.

3. Tell God what you need.
   - Use a simple prayer:

     "God, I just want to be with you."

     "God, I need your guidance."

     "Lord, I want to feel your love."

4. Use Scripture to listen to God.

- Invite God to speak to you through his Word (Psalm 23 is included below).

- Read it slowly and deliberately, as though you were reading a love letter from God to you.

- Notice the words or phrases that stand out and speak to your heart.

- In which of the scenes described in this psalm do you see yourself?

- What thoughts or emotions surface as you see yourself there?

- Which aspects of the Lord as a caring shepherd do you most need or desire at this time?

> The LORD is my shepherd, I shall not be in want.
>   He makes me lie down in green pastures,
> he leads me beside quiet waters,
>   he restores my soul.
> He guides me in paths of righteousness
>   for his name's sake.
> Even though I walk
>   through the valley of the shadow of death,
> I will fear no evil,
>   for you are with me;
> your rod and your staff,
>   they comfort me.
> You prepare a table before me
>   in the presence of my enemies.
> You anoint my head with oil;
>   my cup overflows.
> Surely goodness and love will follow me
>   all the days of my life,
> and I will dwell in the house of the LORD
>   forever.
>
> (Psalm 23)

SOLITUDE

5. Be fully present.
   - Remind yourself that you just need to be yourself with God.
   - Give him your undivided attention.
   - Anticipate distractions by:

     —ignoring them

     —writing them down on a piece of paper for later

     —incorporating them right into your prayers.
   - Speak to him directly about whatever you are thinking or feeling—anger, gratitude, boredom, joy, sadness, need.

6. Respond to what you hear God saying to you through Scripture or in prayer.
   - Speak to God about what you have sensed and felt and heard. Do this verbally or by writing.
   - You could start your journal entry with the words, "God, what I hear you saying to me is …" Then fill in what you're hearing. Follow up with, "This makes me feel …"

7. Express gratitude and commitment.
   - Spend a few minutes thanking God for his presence with you.
   - Express your commitment to respond faithfully to whatever it is you have heard from him during this time.

INDIVIDUAL ACTIVITY

Experiencing Solitude

Notes:

SOLITUDE

Summary

Listen and speak to God in times of solitude.

Your relationship with God will grow significantly deeper.

SPIRITUAL PATHWAYS

SPIRITUAL PATHWAYS

What Is a Spiritual Pathway?

A spiritual pathway is the way we most naturally connect with God and grow spiritually.

We tend to favor one or two main pathways.

There is usually at least one pathway that is very unnatural for us.

The goal is for you to feel great _____ and joy in using it.

If you don't identify and develop your spiritual pathway, it will be very difficult to experience God's presence with you in an ordinary day.

INDIVIDUAL ACTIVITY

Spiritual Pathway Assessment

1. Respond to each statement below according to the following scale:

   3 = Consistently/definitely true of me

   2 = Often/usually true of me

   1 = Once in a while/sometimes true of me

   0 = Not at all/never true of me

   Put the number in the blank before each statement.

2. Transfer the numbers you gave for each assessment statement to the grid on page 71.

3. Total each column. The highest number identifies your preferred spiritual pathway; the next highest number, your secondary pathway.

_3_ *1. When I have a problem, I'd rather pray with people than pray alone.*

_3_ *2. In a church service, I most look forward to the teaching.*

_2_ *3. People who know me would describe me as enthusiastic during worship times.*

_2_ *4. No matter how tired I get, I usually come alive when a challenge is placed before me.*

_3_ *5. Spiritual reality sometimes feels more real to me than the physical world.*

0   6.   *I get distracted in meetings or services if I notice details in the surroundings that haven't been attended to.*

2   7.   *A beautiful sunset can give me a spiritual high that temporarily blocks out everything bothering me.*

3   8.   *It makes me feel better about myself to hang out with people I know and like.*

3   9.   *I've never understood why people don't love to study the Bible in depth.*

3   10.   *God touches me every time I gather with other believers for praise.*

3   11.   *People around me know how passionate I feel about the causes I'm involved in.*

2   12.   *I experience a deep inner joy when I am in a quiet place, free from distractions.*

3   13.   *Helping others is easy for me, even when I have problems.*

2   14.   *When faced with a difficult decision, I am drawn to walk in the woods, on the beach, or in some other outdoor setting.*

3   15.   *When I am alone too much, I tend to lose energy or get a little depressed.*

2   16.   *People seek me out when they need answers to biblical questions.*

3   17.   *Even when I'm tired, I look forward to going to a church service.*

3   18.   *I sense the presence of God most when I'm doing his work.*

0   19.   *I don't understand how Christians can be so busy and still think they're hearing from God.*

1   20.   *I love being able to serve behind the scenes, out of the spotlight.*

0   21.   *I experience God in nature so powerfully I'm sometimes tempted not to bother with church.*

3 22. I experience God most tangibly in fellowship with a few others.

3 23. When I need to be refreshed, a stimulating book is just the thing.

3 24. I am happiest when I praise God together with others.

3 25. "When the going gets tough, the tough get going"—that's true about me!

0 26. My family and friends sometimes tease me about being such a hermit.

3 27. People around me sometimes tell me they admire my compassion.

0 28. Things in nature often teach me valuable lessons about God.

3 29. I don't understand people who have a hard time revealing personal things about themselves.

2 30. Sometimes I spend too much time learning about an issue rather than dealing with it.

3 31. I don't think there's any good excuse for missing a worship time.

2 32. I get tremendous satisfaction from seeing people working together to achieve a goal.

1 33. When I face a difficulty, being alone feels most helpful.

2 34. Even when I'm tired, I find I have the energy and desire to care for people's problems.

2 35. God is so real when I'm in a beautiful, natural setting.

3 36. When I'm tired, there's nothing better than going out with friends to refresh me.

3 37. I worship best in response to theological truth clearly explained.

3 38. I like how all the world's problems—including mine—seem unimportant when I'm praising God at church.

[ ] 39. I get frustrated with people's apathy in the face of injustice.

[0] 40. If the truth were told, I sometimes feel guilty for enjoying silence and solitude so much.

[2] 41. I am happiest when I find someone who really needs help and I step in and offer it.

[0] 42. Others know that if I'm not around, I'm most likely outside in a beautiful place.

[3] 43. People around me describe me as a people person.

[2] 44. I often read lots of books or articles to help me work through a problem.

[3] 45. When I get overwhelmed, there's nothing like a good worship service to get me back on track.

[3] 46. I should probably take more time to slow down, but I really love what I do, especially ministry.

[1] 47. Sometimes I spend too much time mulling over negative things people say about me.

[3] 48. I experience God's presence as I counsel someone who is struggling or in trouble.

[2] 49. When I see natural beauty, something wonderful stirs in me that is difficult to describe.

SESSION SIX

Spiritual Pathway Assessment Scoring

Transfer the numbers from the assessment to this grid, and total each column.

1. 3	2. 3	3. 2	4. 2	5. 3	6. 0	7. 2
8. 3	9. 3	10. 3	11. 3	12. 2	13. 3	14. 2
15. 3	16. 2	17. 3	18. 3	19. 0	20. 1	21. 0
22. 3	23. 3	24. 3	25. 3	26. 0	27. 3	28. 0
29. 3	30. 2	31. 3	32. 2	33. 1	34. 2	35. 2
36. 2	37. 3	38. 3	39. 1	40. 0	41. 2	42. 0
43. 3	44. 2	45. 3	46. 3	47. 1	48. 3	49. 2
Total 20	Total 18	Total 20	Total 17	Total 7	Total 14	Total 8
A Relational	B Intellectual	C Worship	D Activist	E Contemplative	F Serving	G Creation
1	2	1	2			

SPIRITUAL PATHWAYS

✓	Relational—I connect best to God when I am with others.	A
✓	Intellectual—I connect best to God when I learn.	B
✓	Worship—I connect best to God when I worship.	C
✓	Activist—I connect best to God when doing great things.	D
	Contemplative—I connect best to God in silence.	E
✓	Serving—I connect best to God while completing Kingdom tasks.	F
	Creation—I connect best to God in nature.	G

Seven Spiritual Pathways*

- Intellectual — *Like to*

- Relational

- Serving

- Worship

- Activist

- Contemplative

- Creation

* For a complete discussion of these and other spiritual pathways, see Gary Thomas, *Sacred Pathways* (Grand Rapids: Zondervan, 2000).

Intellectual

Characteristics

You draw close to God as you're able to learn more about him.

The study of _____*Scripture*_____ and theology comes naturally.

You have little patience for emotional approaches to faith.

You are a thinker.

When you face problems or spiritual challenges, you go into problem-solving mode.

Biblical Example

The Apostle Paul

Other Example

_____

Strengths

Read great books that challenge you.

Expose yourself to lots of teaching.

Find like-minded people with whom you can learn.

Cautions

Guard against becoming all head and no heart.

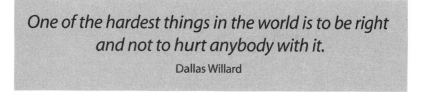

> *One of the hardest things in the world is to be right and not to hurt anybody with it.*
>
> Dallas Willard

Don't confuse being smart with being spiritually mature.

Ways to Stretch

Devote yourself to corporate worship and to private adoration and prayer.

Your learning needs to lead to _____Worship_____; otherwise it will get dangerous.

> *Knowledge puffs up, but love builds up.*
>
> (1 Corinthians 8:1b)

Engage in self-examination to assess whether or not you are being loving.

Relational

Characteristics

Spiritual growth comes most naturally when you're involved in significant _relationships_ .

Small groups and other community life experiences are key.

Your life is an open book.

Being alone can drive you crazy.

In key times of growth, God will often speak to you through people.

Biblical Example

The Apostle Peter

Other Example

_____

Strengths

You need a relationally rich life.

Use your spiritual gift to serve others.

Pray with others in community.

Learn in a class with other people or in a small group.

Use your network of contacts to further God's kingdom.

Cautions

Guard against superficiality.

You can grow ___dependent___ on others and become a spiritual chameleon.

Ways to Stretch

Develop a capacity for ___silence___.

Keep some of your experiences with God secret so you don't get addicted to what other people think.

Study Scripture for yourself so you are grounded in God's Word rather than in others' opinions.

Invite close friends to speak truth to you so that your relationship is more than just social.

SPIRITUAL PATHWAYS

Serving

Characteristics

God's presence seems most tangible when you're involved in helping others.

You're often uncomfortable in a setting where you don't have a role. If you have a role, then you sense God's presence and delight.

You constantly look for acts of _____*Service*_____ you can engage in and often don't even need to be asked.

Biblical Example

Dorcas in the Book of Acts

Other Example

_____*Mother Teresa*_____

Strengths

Get plugged into a _____*Community*_____ so you have opportunities for meaningful service to offer God.

Look for glimpses of God's presence in the people you serve and in the execution of your tasks.

Prepare to serve first by praying so your service is genuinely spiritual service.

Cautions

Be careful not to resent other people who don't serve as much as you do.

Remember that God loves you, not because you are so faithful in serving him, but because you are his ___Child___.

Don't confuse serving with earning God's love.

Ways to Stretch

Balance your service with small group and community life.

Learn how to receive love even when you're not being productive.

Practice expressing love through ___Words___ as well as actions.

SPIRITUAL PATHWAYS

Worship

> *I rejoiced with those who said to me,*
> *"Let us go to the house of the LORD."*
> (Psalm 122:1)

Characteristics

You have a deep love of corporate praise and a natural inclination toward celebration.

In difficult periods of life, worship is one of the most healing activities you engage in.

In worship, your _____ hearT _____ opens up, and you come alive and enthusiastically participate.

Biblical Example

King David (wrote alot ot songs)

Other Example

_____

Strengths

Experience great worship on a regular basis.

Use worship tapes or CDs and make your car a private sanctuary.

Learn about other worship traditions, and incorporate what you learn into your personal worship time.

Cautions

Be careful not to judge those who aren't as expressive in worship.

Guard against an experience-based spirituality that always has you looking for the next worship "high."

This is what C.S. Lewis called "the fatal sin of saying 'encore!'"

> *The danger in finding a way to God is that people grow to love the way more than they love God.*
> Meister Eckhart

Ways to Stretch

Engage in the discipline of ___Study___.

Serve God in concrete ways as an extension of your worship.

Remain committed to your church even when worship isn't all you would like it to be.

Activist

Description

You have a single-minded zeal and a very strong sense of

_____Vision_____.

You have a passion to build the church and to work for justice.

Challenges don't discourage you.

You do everything you can to bring out the _potential_
God has placed in other people.

You love a fast-paced, problem-filled, complex, strenuous way of life.

Biblical Example

Nehemiah

William & Catherine Booth (Salvation Army)

> *I prayed to the God of heaven, and I answered the king.*
> (Nehemiah 2:4b-5a)

Prayer and action go hand in hand for the activist.

Other Example

_____

Strengths

Create a sense of _____*Challenge*_____ in your life by immersing yourself in tasks that call out the best you have to offer.

> ## When I run, I feel God's pleasure.
> Eric Liddel, *Chariots of Fire*

Find a team of people you can invest in and work with to accomplish big goals.

Cautions

You may run over people or use them because you get so focused on achieving the goal.

Guard against going too long without pausing to reflect on what you're doing.

You can end up not even knowing your own ___*motives*___, spiritual condition, or emotional state.

Ways to Stretch

Spend time in solitude and silence.

Cultivate a reflective discipline like journaling. (It is an *action.*)

Develop close spiritual friendships with one or two other people.

Invite them to:

—regularly ask you questions.

—speak to you about what God is doing *in* you, not just *through* you.

These relationships must be focused on you, not on tasks.

Contemplative - *Lowest Score*

Characteristics

You love uninterrupted _time alone_.

Reflection comes naturally to you.

You have a large capacity for prayer.

If you get busy or spend a lot of time with people, you feel drained and yearn for times of solitude.

Biblical Example

Mary, Martha's sister (Luke 10:38-42)

Other Example

_____

Strengths

(Note: You have *permission* to build on your strengths!)

You need regular, protected, intense times of solitude and stillness.

Faithfully follow the intuitions and leadings that come in your times alone with God.

Act on what you hear from God in the silence."

Cautions

You have a tendency to avoid the demands of the real world because it doesn't live up to your ideals.

Be careful not to retreat to your inner world when friends, family, or society disappoint you.

Resist the temptation to consider your times of private prayer and solitude as less important than the more public acts of ministry performed by others.

Ways to Stretch

Choose a regular place of active service.

Stay relationally connected, even when those relationships become difficult or challenging.

Connect with those who have an activist pathway.

—Pray for them.

—Consider getting involved in some aspect of their ministry activities.

Creation   — *Low Score*

Characteristics

You respond deeply to God through your experience of

_____ *nature* _____.

Being outdoors replenishes you.

You're highly aware of your physical senses, and often art, or symbols, or ritual will help you grow.

You tend to be creative.

Biblical Example

Jesus

Other Example

_____

Strengths

Spend time _____ *out doors* _____.

Find a location for getaways.

Make beauty a part of your spiritual life.

Cautions

You may be tempted to use beauty or nature to escape.

You will find that people are sometimes disappointing.

Guard against the temptation to avoid church because you think to yourself, "I can worship God in nature, on my own."

Ways to Stretch

Stay involved in a worshiping community.

Be willing to help out in less-than-beautiful settings.

Take Scripture with you into nature, and meditate on God's Word as you enjoy his creation.

SPIRITUAL PATHWAYS

Developing My Spiritual Pathway

Based on what you've learned about your preferred spiritual pathway, answer the following questions:

What are one or two activities you need to engage in regularly to stay connected with God?

Reading bible.

How might you incorporate these activities into your daily or weekly routine?

Read Christian Books

Which pathway is a stretch for you but might help you connect with God in new ways?

Making the Most of Your Spiritual Pathway

Give yourself permission to be who you are in God. Celebrate it!

Engage in activities that move you out of your comfort zone.

Be careful not to envy someone else's pathway.

Beware the temptation to _____Judge_____ someone else because of his or her pathway.

Explore and develop the other pathways.

SPIRITUAL PATHWAYS

Summary

Each of us has one or two preferred spiritual pathways.

It's good to explore *all* the spiritual pathways.

SESSION SEVEN

PACE OF

LIFE

PACE OF LIFE

Hurry Sickness

Do You Have Hurry Sickness?

1. You go through your day with a constant sense of urgency.

Not at all like me — Like me sometimes — Describes me most of the time

●————————————————X————————————————●

2. You notice underlying tension in close relationships.

Not at all like me — Like me sometimes — Describes me most of the time

●————————————————X————————————————●

3. You have a preoccupation with escaping.

Not at all like me — Like me sometimes — Describes me most of the time

●————X————————————————————————————●

4. You often feel frustrated because you're not getting things done.

Not at all like me — Like me sometimes — Describes me most of the time

●————————————————X————————————————●

5. You sense that time is passing too quickly without you getting what you really want out of life.

Not at all like me   Like me sometimes   Describes me most of the time

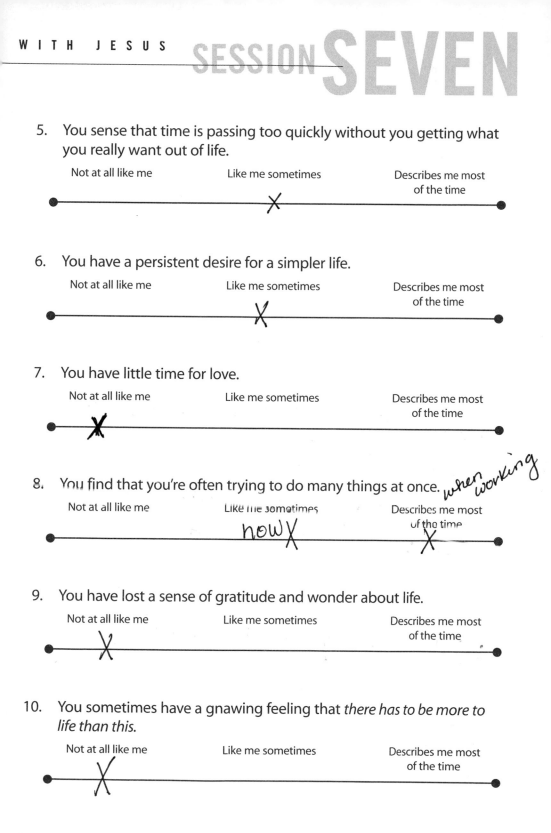

6. You have a persistent desire for a simpler life.

Not at all like me   Like me sometimes   Describes me most of the time

7. You have little time for love.

Not at all like me   Like me sometimes   Describes me most of the time

8. You find that you're often trying to do many things at once. *when working*

Not at all like me   Like me sometimes *now*   Describes me most of the time

9. You have lost a sense of gratitude and wonder about life.

Not at all like me   Like me sometimes   Describes me most of the time

10. You sometimes have a gnawing feeling that *there has to be more to life than this.*

Not at all like me   Like me sometimes   Describes me most of the time

PACE OF LIFE

The Price of Hurry Sickness

1. Review your responses to the ten questions on the Hurry Sickness Inventory on pages 92–93. Which question and response has the greatest "ouch" factor for you? Circle that one.

2. Reflect on the following questions and then write your responses in the spaces below.

   What problems arise—or affect those you love—because you are hurried?

   In past when working I spent Sat working time away from them. Mostly after kids raised.

   What price are you paying for hurry sickness?

   don't enjoy the moment.

Two Big Illusions

1. Time: "Someday, things will settle down."

   You must ruthlessly eliminate ___the hurry___ from your life.

   Hurry is the great enemy of spiritual life.

   The difference between being *busy* and being *hurried:*

   Busy has to do with our outward condition.

   Hurry:

   —has to do with the state of our ___souls___.

   —is an inward condition that results from having too many competing priorities in any given moment.

   Jesus was often ___busy___, but he was never hurried.

2. Stuff: "Someday, 'more' will be enough."

   The distance between more and enough is an unbridgeable chasm.

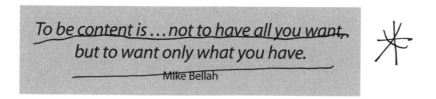

> *To be content is ... not to have all you want,*
> *but to want only what you have.*
> — Mike Bellah

PACE OF LIFE

Five Training Activities

Five training activities you can do during ordinary days to simplify your life and align yourself with God's priorities:

1. Slowing

    Walk more slowly.

    Chew your food.

    Breathe deeply.

    X Really listen to children.

    X Drive in the slow lane.

    Get in the longest line at the grocery store.

2. Saying no

    Every commitment is a decision that helps or hinders our ability to love God and others.

    Every time we say yes to one thing, we are saying no to something else.

3. Keep the ___Sabbath Day___.

Commit to one day a week when you rest and do no work.

Take a long walk.

Read a spiritually enriching book.

Have an unhurried conversation.

Avoid certain activities (reading advertisements or checking e-mail).

Thank God for the gift of a Sabbath.

Engage in activities that are restful and renewing.

4. (De-clutter)

The more stuff we have, the more time and energy are required to maintain it.

What could you live without in order to simplify your life?

Go through your closet, basement, and garage—give things away.

5. Use leisure time in ___lifegiving___ ways.

gives energy & joy

Choose activities that refresh.

Incorporate your spiritual pathway into your schedule.

— do not eat
— take a walk
— Read bible

PACE OF LIFE

INDIVIDUAL ACTIVITY

Letting God Speak

1) relax ~~peace~~ <u>Listen</u> to Danis, Taylor, Delbert, Michelle, Candace

Will have peace.

Be in word.

Summary

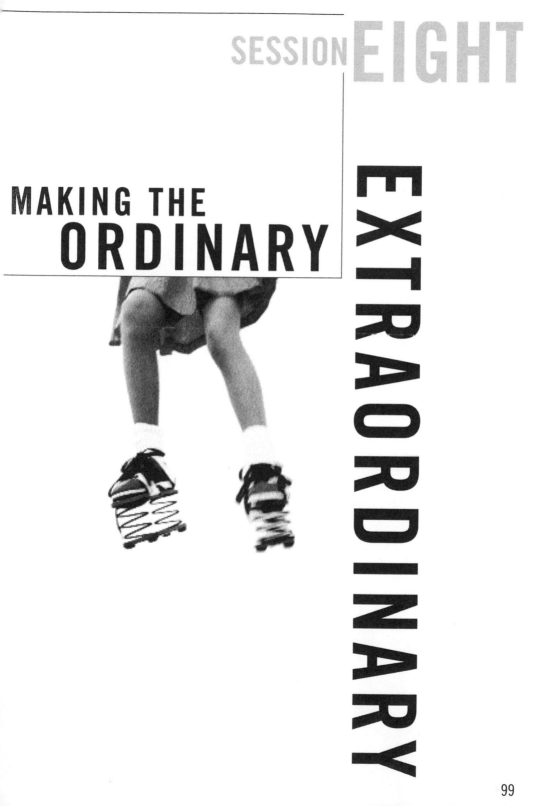

SESSION EIGHT

MAKING THE
ORDINARY

EXTRAORDINARY

MAKING THE ORDINARY EXTRAORDINARY

Three Issues

1. Belief

   You must honestly believe that experiencing the reality of God in your everyday life is a real possibility.

   Key question: Do I really believe this is possible for *me?*

   > *The kingdom of God is near.*
   > (Mark 1:15)

   Believe it!

2. Desire

   We must grow in our desire for this kind of life.

   > *We must journey to find the life we prize*
   > *and the guide we have been given*
   > *is the desire set deep within.*
   > John Eldredge

   Key question: Do I really want Jesus to accompany me through every moment of my day?

   The truth about us never scares Jesus.

3. Decision

There is a big difference between desiring to do something and actually doing it. The difference is a decision.

Key question: What am I willing to *do* so my desires come to pass?

MY ORDINARY DAY (date:

PART OF THE DAY	HOW I WANT TO DO THIS IN JESUS' NAME	EXAMPLES FROM THE COURSE
The Night Before	- Devotion before bedtime - Prayer	• Get enough sleep. • Resolve conflicts before going to bed. • Invite Jesus to be with you when you wake. • Review the day with God.
Waking Up	- Devotion - Prayer for day	• Renew your invitation to Jesus. • Speak to Jesus about any anxieties or concerns you feel. • Acknowledge your dependence on Jesus.
Morning Routine/Breakfast	- Exercise - make breakfast home.	• Greet members of your household differently. • See *Using Meal Times as Mini-Breaks*, page 118.
During the Workday (remember, everyone works!)	- Plan meals for day - Start going through pictures (1 day/wk) ① family. ② church friends & All friends	**WORKING** • Show up on time. • Greet coworkers (or children) differently. • Take a moment to pray. **BREAKS** • Take mini-breaks. • Take a short walk. • Take five to ten minutes to be quiet and focus on God. **LUNCH** • See *Using Meal Times as Mini-Breaks*, page 118. **EVERYDAY RELATIONSHIPS** • Listen. Use the phrase "Tell me more." • Use touch. • Speak words of love. • Look for opportunities to do simple acts of service. • Learn from difficult people. • Receive feedback well. **MISCELLANEOUS** • Place symbols or reminders of God's presence in your work setting. • Make sure your work setting is well ordered.

Category	Handwritten notes	Details
During the Workday *(continued)*		• Walk more slowly. • Breathe deeply. • Drive in the slow lane. • Stand in the longest line at the grocery store. **ENDING THE WORKDAY** • Focus on what you have done and declare it good. • End your day honestly. Ask God for help to work diligently the next day.
Dinner/ Evening Routine		• See *Using Meal Times as Mini-Breaks*, page 118. • See "Everyday Relationships" above.
Miscellaneous	Read Christian Books	**LEADINGS** • Listen for God's leadings and follow them. **SOLITUDE** • Schedule a time to be alone with God. **SPIRITUAL PATHWAYS** • Use your strenghts; incorporate activities that help you stay connected with God. • Be willing to stretch; incorporate activities that move you out of your comfort zone. **PACE OF LIFE** • Declutter; Clean out your closet, basement, or garage and give things away. • Use leisure time in life-giving ways. • Set appropriate boundaries by saying no to some things so you can say yes to others.
Sabbath Day	Church nap in afternoon	• Keep the Sabbath: Choose and commit to one day a week to rest and do no work. • Take a long walk. • Get extra sleep. • Read a spiritually enriching book. • Have an unhurried conversation. • Create time for prayer and solitude. • Avoid certain activities: checking e-mail, reading advertisements, etc.

MAKING THE ORDINARY EXTRAORDINARY

Two Things to Keep in Mind

1. Don't be defeated by "failure."

   Don't worry about a missed moment—there's another one coming right after it.

2. Don't forget to look for "burning bushes."

   Be ready to turn aside and notice when God does unexpected things in your day.

An Ordinary Day with Jesus

Notes:

INDIVIDUAL ACTIVITY

Letter to God

1. Reflect on the ways in which God has spoken to you throughout this course.

   - Do you really believe it is possible for you to spend an ordinary day with Jesus?

   - Do you really want Jesus to accompany you through every moment of the day?

   - What are you willing to do so your desires come to pass?

2. In the space on the next page, write a letter to God expressing your belief, desire, and decision, as well as any questions or fears. Be completely honest.

3. Commit your ordinary day plan to him.

4. Close your letter with an expression of gratitude for God's presence with you now and in the days to come.

MAKING THE ORDINARY EXTRAORDINARY
Letter to God

- thank you God for loving me and wanting to be with me every day in every way.
- Help me to Love you most and Love others by really Listening to them.
- Devotions morning & night
- Pray Journal
- Not be hurried & Listen to God. Be aware of His Wisdom coming to me.
- take care self - food & exercise

Course Summary

God calls us to the challenge and privilege to do all of life in Jesus' name.

It's not a matter of *trying* harder but of *training* to become like Christ.

He invites us to join with him throughout the day.

He invites us to listen for his leadings and to spend time alone with him.

He gives each of us at least one unique spiritual pathway to connect with him.

He calls us to let go of the illusions that *someday* we'll have time for him or *someday* we'll have the stuff we need to be happy.

Instead he says now—in our ordinary days—that *this* is the time and place for us to know and enjoy him.

Remember, there is no failure.

Course Evaluation

1. To what extent did this course meet your expectations?

5	4	3	2	1
Went beyond expectations		Met expectations		Less than expected

2. How much learning did you experience during this course?

5	4	3	2	1
Significant		Moderate		Little

3. How relevant is what you learned to your daily life?

5	4	3	2	1
Highly relevant		Somewhat relevant		Not relevant

4. Would you recommend that others attend this course?

5	4	3	2	1
Yes, definitely		Possibly		Definitely not

COURSE EVALUATION

5. **What aspects of this course were most useful and/or meaningful?**

6. **What aspects of this course were least useful and/or meaningful?**

7. **What, if anything, would you like to change about this course?**

8. **To what extent did the instructor demonstrate depth of understanding and credibility with regard to the material?**

5	4	3	2	1
To a very great extent		To some extent		To little or no extent

9. **To what extent did the instructor have a motivating effect, contributing to your learning?**

5	**4**	**3**	**2**	**1**
To a very great extent		To some extent		To little or no extent

10. **Additional comments:**

APPENDIX

Steps to Grow through Conflict

We all experience relational conflict. To be alive means to be in conflict. Sometimes we'd rather pretend conflict doesn't exist or that a lack of conflict is a sign of spiritual maturity. *But conflict is normal.* Everybody experiences it. Maturity is shown in how you deal with it.

Jesus gives very clear council on steps to take through conflict. He says in Matthew 18:15: "If another believer sins against you, go privately and point out the fault. If the other person listens and confesses it, you have won that person back" (NLT).

Notice the steps. If there is conflict:
    You go …
    to the person …
    privately …
    discuss the problem …
    for the purpose of reconciliation.

We can summarize Jesus' instructions in a single phrase: *go and tell.* The odd thing is, we don't do it—this may be one of the most violated of all Jesus' commands. At each step, we're faced with a crossroads accompanied by powerful reasons to ignore his instructions and go the other way.

Step One: *You Go*

Jesus identifies the first step. He says, *you go.* The implication is clear: *You* take the initiative.

The truth is, we don't want to take initiative. Too often we think, "Let the other person come to *me!* It's not fair that I should have to be the one to take the first step."

If you have been wronged, Jesus puts the burden on you to take the initiative to make it right. If someone has something against you, you take action; if someone has done something to you, Jesus says, *you go.* Be direct, don't avoid the other person in hopes that things will somehow get better on their own.

At this point, it's tempting to balk. "But I don't want to go! I want to stay and stew. I'd rather just be mad. Besides, if I go it may get ugly." The root of the problem is this: We're afraid.

One man was thinking about a confrontation he needed to engage in, and told his wife: "Every time I think about having this confrontation, my palms get sweaty." A little later he said, "Now every time I think about it, my mouth gets dry." So his wife proposed a solution: "Why don't you lick your palms?"

Sweaty palms or dry mouth, we need to address conflict head-on.

Pray for help   See Jesus/God in them.

Step Two: *To the Person*

Step two is, *to the person.* Jesus said go directly to the person—no third parties.

We often think to ourselves, "I don't want to go to the person I'm having conflict with. That's the *last* person I want to go to. I want to go to someone else and say, 'Don't you share my concerns about this sister or brother in Christ—who is a deeply disturbed psychopath?'"

Or we spiritualize our gossip: "I'm only telling you this because I want you to be able to pray more *intelligently.*"

But Jesus says go *to the person,* not someone else.

Step Three: *Privately*

Step three is, *privately*. This means when the two of you are alone. You have to say no to the temptation to embarrass somebody in front of others. Often, we rationalize that there's "safety in numbers"—it's easier to say something hard in a group setting rather than one-on-one. But don't do it. First go *privately*.

Step Four: *Discuss the Problem*

Step four is to point out the fault, which means *discuss the problem*. Use direct communication. Sometimes, in an effort to soften the blow, we end up addressing the problem indirectly.

For instance, sometimes we make a statement that covers up our real feelings. We say, "It's too bad we missed the start of the concert," but what we really mean is, "I'm really angry that you weren't ready when you said you would be—and that made us late!" In the same vein we may say, "You must have really been busy," but we're actually angry that the person consistently fails to be punctual.

A better way is to be honest about our emotions: "I'm really feeling angry right now!" Then ask for what you want and invite a response: "I want you to do what you say you will or next time I'll leave without you. If you've got a better idea, I'm open to it, but I'm not going to allow your delays to spoil my evening." That way the person knows how you feel, what to expect from you, and what options are still open.

Paul echoes this teaching in Ephesians 4:15 when he says to speak the truth in love. He says to be loving—but be sure to speak the truth!

Step Five: *For the Purpose of Reconciliation*

Step five is to win the person back, which means the confrontation is *for the purpose of reconciliation.* Be clear on the goal: to win back the other person and to restore the relationship. It's not just about dumping on the other person, or making them feel bad. It's about moving toward each other.

Conclusion

As you work through these five steps, remember that Jesus taught we should always have a humble spirit, and be keenly aware of the log in our own eye, not just the speck in someone else's (Matthew 7:3-5). We are all flawed, capable of spiritual blindness and pride. We must always look for ways we have contributed to the problem even as we try to help the other person own their part. Keep praying, "God, what do you want to teach me about my shortcomings?"

The next time you need to address conflict, follow these five steps. See if Jesus' way of handling conflict doesn't give you better results than the gossipy, roundabout way our culture tends to do it.

Using Mealtimes as Mini-Breaks

Mealtimes are not just physically nourishing; they can be spiritually nourishing too. Here are some simple ideas for using mealtimes to refresh yourself and those with whom you are eating.

Before eating, take a moment to be genuinely grateful.

If sharing your meal with others, prior to eating ask them how you can pray for them.

Be creative when you pray before eating. Many of us were brought up to think that if we didn't close our eyes during prayer it wouldn't count, but of course that's not true. If you're eating with a spouse or good friend, look right at them as you pray for God to bless them.

Pay attention to the flavor of the food you're eating.

When you eat, slow down. Chew.

If you're with others, seek to bring joy to them. Jesus did this all the time with some pretty unsavory characters—and often got in trouble for it! If you're alone, pray for someone you care about and bring them joy secretly.

Feed on Scripture. Jesus said we don't live by bread alone "but by every word that proceeds from the mouth of God" (Luke 4:4). Select a phrase from Scripture such as "the Lord is my shepherd." As your body feeds on food from God, let your mind feed on the Word of God.

What to Do If You're in a Wrong Job Fit

Discerning a calling or our true vocation often requires time and patience—and most of us have bills that must be paid in the meantime. What can we do while we're still searching for the right job fit? The truth is, there are no easy answers, and virtually all solutions unfold gradually. This is hard news for those of us who want to microwave everything, including our vocations. We may be tempted to jump into—or out of—commitments too rashly.

Author Bob Buford suggests initiating what he calls a "low-cost probe" (see his book *Halftime*). The idea is to keep your day job but test the waters of a new calling. Begin to explore your skills and abilities in the area where you feel God may be calling. In Buford's case, the low-cost probe meant retaining his CEO position while pulling together a group of pastors to see if they could benefit from the organizational expertise he'd acquired in his business career. What he discovered led to a new calling for the second half of his life. But the cost was low enough that, had it been a dead end, he could easily have turned his search elsewhere. Had he impulsively quit his job and taken a staff position at a church, he might have missed his calling and jeopardized his ability to keep searching.

Maybe for you a low-cost probe would involve a short-term mission trip, taking on a commitment to teach at your church, volunteering, or working somewhere part-time. There's actually biblical precedent for this type of two-track career exploration. Amos transitioned into the prophecy business but still had his shepherding position to fall back on. The Apostle Paul apparently kept his tent-making business while he simultaneously went into church planting.

In his book *In Time of Choice*, author Gordon Smith notes that God often honors our previous decisions and commitments. God is a careful worker and, like any other careful worker, he's not likely to waste any resources. The competencies and skills you've acquired to this point in your life matter to him, and may be squandered if you make a rash decision to leave your current situation. So while God may have a new direction for you, consider how he might "recycle" the training and expertise you've accumulated so far.

A Simple Plan for Solitude

Solitude is not a complicated practice. In fact, if you make it complicated, you work against the very simplicity and quietness it is intended to foster. Here are a few simple steps to help you eliminate unwanted distractions, and plan your solitude time for maximum effectiveness.

1. *Find a quiet place that is free of distractions*

Remember the video, shown early in the session, where the woman was trying to pray in the midst of her hectic day? One of the problems she faced was giving God her undivided attention in a setting filled with distractions:

> toys and clothing that begged to be picked up
> a phone waiting to interrupt her
> a TV crying to be turned on
> a dryer buzzer screaming to be attended to

She also hadn't clearly set apart the time for her and God, so she felt pulled by her desire to use the time in other ways.

Although we might not always be able to find the perfect setting, solitude requires getting away from the normal distractions of our lives. It requires a time frame in which we can be with God in an unhurried way. You will need to identify a time in the context of your ordinary day when you can give God your undivided attention on a regular basis.

People often find it helpful to identify what they might call a "sacred space"—a place set apart for meeting with God and God alone. It is important that you bring very little with you into this space—perhaps just a Bible and a journal. You may even want to personalize this space by incorporating a symbol that reminds you of God's presence with you. You could use a special Scripture verse or poem, a lit candle to remind you of the presence of the Holy Spirit, a cross or a thorn to remind you of Christ's sacrificial love for you.

Your space needs to be relatively free of distractions so you can give God your undivided attention—a special chair, a corner of your office or bedroom, a spot on your porch or in your backyard (if weather permits). Depending on your stage of life, you might have to resort to a closet or your car!

As much as possible, make this a nonnegotiable time in your schedule. You may need to communicate this to others in your household so they will be able to honor those times when you are alone with God.

2. *Quiet yourself in God's presence*
Interpersonal interactions rarely develop into meaningful communication when we rush in breathless and distracted. We need some time at the beginning to slow down.

Take a few moments to quiet yourself by breathing deeply, giving yourself a chance to slow down and become aware of God's presence with you. If you are distracted, make a list of your concerns and then set it aside so you can be fully present with God.

3. *Tell God what you need*
Tell God what you would like to receive from him during your time together. It may be that you need encouragement, to feel his forgiveness, wisdom for a decision, reassurance of his love. Be yourself. Let God know what is on your heart and invite him to give you what he already knows you need. You may find it helpful to use a brief prayer such as, "Here I am," or "Jesus Christ, have mercy on me," or "Come, Lord Jesus," to express your openness to God and your desire to receive whatever he has to give.

4. *Use Scripture to listen to God*
Approach Scripture prayerfully, inviting God to speak to you. You might begin with the prayer that the little boy Samuel prayed: "Speak, Lord, for your servant is listening." Read slowly and deliberately, listening for what God has to say to you through his Word. Rather than skimming the Bible

like you might skim the newspaper, approach it as you would a letter from someone you love deeply—and who deeply loves you.

Imagine yourself in the passage or in the setting of the story you are reading. Ask questions that help you reflect on the meaning of the passage for your own life:

Where do I see myself in this passage?

Which character do I relate to most?

What thoughts or emotions surface as I envision myself there?

Which aspect of what is being said here do I need or desire most?

What is most challenging?

5. Be fully present

One of the most important things you can do to be fully present with God is to be yourself. The woman in the video had trouble with this. She seemed to feel that she had to censor her truest feelings about her life, her husband, and her friends. No wonder her times with God felt like an obligation rather than an opportunity.

Sometimes we fall into the trap of only praying about "spiritual-sounding" things, as if God didn't know all our thoughts anyway! This is deadly to prayer. C. S. Lewis wrote that we must speak to God "what is in us, not what *ought* to be in us."

Being fully present involves knowing what to do with distractions. The truth is that all of us struggle from S-A-D-D or "spiritual attention deficit disorder" from time to time. There are several things you can do to bring yourself back to your intent to be fully present with God. If your wandering thoughts really do seem like a distraction—like a to-do list— you can jot them down and then let them go, knowing that you can return to them at an appropriate time.

Some distractions, though, are not distractions at all; they could be promptings from the Holy Spirit. What we often think of as distractions might be thoughts and feelings we need to bring to God in prayer. Then we need to listen for what he has to say about them. The woman in the video could have done this with her feelings about her husband. Rather than dismissing her feelings of frustration about her husband and pretending that they were different than they were, she could have shared her feelings with God and asked him for truth and wisdom about what she should do with them.

If you give some thought to how you want to handle distractions before you begin your time in solitude, you can deal with them and still remain fully present with God.

6. *Respond to what you hear God saying to you through Scripture or in prayer*

Speak to God about what you are sensing, feeling, and hearing. Some people find it helpful to respond verbally in prayer while others write out their prayers in a journal. Experiment by addressing God as if you were writing a letter, or writing what you think God is saying to you.

If you choose to write your prayers, it is important to do so without censoring yourself. Sometimes people burn their journals when they are full to make sure they are free to be totally honest rather than afraid that someone else will read their words. However, if you keep your journals, over time they can become a rich history of your private times with God.

7. *Express gratitude and commitment*

Close your time in solitude by thanking God for his presence with you. Let him know you intend to respond faithfully to whatever you heard from him—and then do it.

Additional Ideas for Simplifying Your Pace of Life

Slowing

Deliberately drive in the slow lane for a day.

Chew your food slowly, putting down the utensil after every bite.

Focus for a day on listening more than speaking.

Pause for several breaks during the day.

Leave your watch off for a day.

Saying No

Skip lunch one day—say no to a meal and devote that time to prayer or journaling about your pace of life.

Keep a log of how you spend your time during a typical week. Ask someone to review it with you, looking for activities to eliminate.

Look in the mirror in the morning and watch yourself say "no," politely but firmly ten times. Then say no to something that day.

What is an activity or involvement you might stop doing eventually? Could you stop doing it now?

Cancel a magazine subscription, knowing you can start it up again in a few months if you really miss it.

Keep the Sabbath

Pick one day and devote it to nonwork. Instead, spend it remembering and thanking God.

Engage in activities that are life-giving to you.

Do one thing that is quite out of the ordinary for you.

Don't do one thing that you would typically do. For example, don't read any advertisements, don't check your e-mail, don't go shopping, etc.

Create time for prayer and solitude within this day.

De-clutter

Have a throw–away day. Ask every member of your household to fill a large garbage bag with stuff to give or throw away.

Go through one drawer in your house and organize it. If you have time, do another.

Go through your freezer and eat everything that's in it before you buy any more frozen foods—this includes ice cream!

Any time you receive a telemarketing call, ask to be removed from their list.

Throw away junk mail without opening it.

Use Leisure Time in Life-Giving Ways

Limit how much TV you watch—budget a certain number of hours per family member per week.

Go for a weekend or a whole week without TV—try a "media fast."

Make a list of twenty-five things you like to do other than watch TV. Do all of those things at least once within six months.

Invite to dinner a few people you really enjoy. Ask each one to bring pictures of themselves as teenagers. Tell stories of what you were like back then.

What is something you liked to do when you were a child? (Examples: fly a kite, dress up dolls, play board games, make a model, paint with watercolors, make a fort with blankets.) Plan to do it this weekend.

Who is someone you would like to do an outrageously kind act for? Send that person a note, do some work at their house, watch their kids, give them some money for no reason, surprise them with a gift, or come up with your own way to use a little of your free time to serve them. Does this leave you replenished or exhausted?

Additional Resources

SESSION 1: LIVING IN JESUS' NAME

The Imitation of Christ, Thomas á Kempis (Ave Maria Press, 1989)
Life Together, Dietrich Bonhoeffer (HarperCollins, 1954, 1978)
Living in the Presence, Tilden Edwards (HarperCollins, 1987, 1995)
The Practice of the Presence of God, Brother Lawrence (Whitaker House, 1982)
The Sacrament of the Present Moment, Jean-Pierre De Caussade (HarperCollins, 1989)

SESSION 2: EVERYDAY RELATIONSHIPS

Connecting, Larry Crabb (Word Books, 1997)
Family the Forming Center, revised edition, Marjorie J. Thompson (Upper Room, 1997)
Friends and Strangers, Karen Burton Mains (Word Books, 1990)
Life Together, Dietrich Bonhoeffer (HarperCollins, 1954, 1978)
Listening for Heaven's Sake, Gary R. Sweeten (Equipping Ministries International, 1993)
The Mystery of Marriage, Mike Mason (Multnomah Publishers, 1985, 1996)
Practicing the Presence of People, Mike Mason (Waterbrook Press, 1999)
The Safest Place on Earth, Larry Crabb (Word Books, 1999)

SESSION 3: WORK

Honest to God? (chapter 11), Bill Hybels (Zondervan, 1990)
Let Your Life Speak, Parker J. Palmer (Jossey-Bass, 1999)
Why You Can't Be Anything You Want to Be, Arthur F. Miller (Zondervan, 1999)
Your Work Matters to God, Doug Sherman and William Hendricks (NavPress, 1987)

ADDITIONAL RESOURCES

SESSION 4: LEADINGS

Hearing God (previously published as *In Search of Guidance*), Dallas
    Willard (InterVarsity Press, 1999)
A Testament of Devotion, Thomas R. Kelly (HarperCollins, 1941, 1996)

SESSION 5: SOLITUDE

Answering God, Eugene H. Peterson (HarperCollins, 1991)
The Genesee Diary, Henri J.M. Nouwen (1981)
The Life of the Beloved, Henri J.M. Nouwen (Crossroad, 1992)
Love Beyond Reason, John Ortberg (Zondervan, 2000)
Prayer, Richard J. Foster (HarperCollins, 1992)
A Spiritual Formation Journal, Jana Rea with Richard J. Foster
    (HarperCollins, 1996)
Too Busy Not to Pray, Bill Hybels (InterVarsity Press, 1998)
The Way of the Heart, Henri J.M. Nouwen (Ballantine Books, 1991)

SESSION 6: SPIRITUAL PATHWAYS

Invitation to a Journey, M. Robert Mulholland (InterVarsity Press, 1993)
Sacred Pathways, Gary Thomas (Zondervan, 2000)
Windows of the Soul, Ken Gire (Zondervan, 1996)

SESSION 7: PACE OF LIFE

Freedom of Simplicity, Richard J. Foster (HarperCollins, 1981, 1998)
Margin, Richard A. Swenson (NavPress, 1992, 1995)
Practicing Our Faith, Dorothy Bass, editor (Jossey-Bass, 1997)
Sabbath Time, Tilden Edwards (Upper Room, 1992)

SESSION 8: MAKING THE ORDINARY EXTRAORDINARY

The Divine Conspiracy, Dallas Willard (HarperCollins, 1998)
If You Want to Walk on Water, You've Got to Get Out of the Boat, John
    Ortberg (Zondervan, 2001)
The Life You've Always Wanted, John Ortberg (Zondervan, 1997)
Receiving the Day, Dorothy Bass (Jossey-Bass, 1999)
The Spirit of the Disciplines, Dallas Willard (HarperCollins, 1991)

Willow Creek Association

Vision, Training, Resources for Prevailing Churches

This resource was created to serve you and to help you build a local church that prevails. It is just one of many ministry tools that are part of the Willow Creek Resources® line, published by the Willow Creek Association together with Zondervan.

The Willow Creek Association (WCA) was created in 1992 to serve a rapidly growing number of churches from across the denominational spectrum that are committed to helping unchurched people become fully devoted followers of Christ. Membership in the WCA now numbers over 10,000 Member Churches worldwide from more than ninety denominations.

The Willow Creek Association links like-minded Christian leaders with each other and with strategic vision, training, and resources in order to help them build prevailing churches designed to reach their redemptive potential. Here are some of the ways the WCA does that.

- **Prevailing Church Conference** — an annual two-and-a-half day event, held at Willow Creek Community Church in South Barrington, Illinois, to help pioneering church leaders raise up a volunteer core while discovering new and innovative ways to build prevailing churches that reach unchurched people.

- **Leadership Summit** — a once-a-year, two-and-a-half-day conference to envision and equip Christians with leadership gifts and responsibilities. Presented live at Willow Creek as well as via satellite broadcast to over sixty locations across North America, this event is designed to increase the leadership effectiveness of pastors, ministry staff, volunteer church leaders, and Christians in the marketplace.

- **Ministry-Specific Conferences** — throughout each year the WCA hosts a variety of conferences and training events — both at Willow Creek's main campus and offsite, across the U.S. and around the world—targeting church leaders in ministry-specific areas such as: evangelism, the arts, children, students, small groups, preaching and teaching, spiritual formation, spiritual gifts, raising up resources, etc.

WILLOW CREEK ASSOCIATION

- **Willow Creek Resources®** — to provide churches with trusted and field-tested ministry resources in such areas as leadership, evangelism, spiritual formation, spiritual gifts, small groups, stewardship, student ministry, children's ministry, the use of the arts — drama, media, contemporary music — and more. For additional information about Willow Creek Resources® call the Customer Service Center at 800-570-9812. Outside the U.S. call 847-765-0070.

- *WillowNet* — the WCA's Internet resource service, which provides access to hundreds of transcripts of Willow Creek messages, drama scripts, songs, videos, and multimedia tools. The system allows users to sort through these elements and download them for a fee. Visit us online at www.willowcreek.com.

- *WCA News* — a quarterly publication to inform you of the latest trends, resources, and information on WCA events from around the world.

- *Defining Moments* — a monthly audio journal for church leaders featuring Bill Hybels and other Christian leaders discussing probing issues to help you discover biblical principles and transferable strategies to maximize your church's redemptive potential.

- *The Exchange* — our online classified ads service to assist churches in recruiting key staff for ministry positions.

- **Member Benefits** — includes substantial discounts to WCA training events, a 20 percent discount on all Willow Creek Resources®, access to a Members-Only section on WillowNet, monthly communications, and more. Member Churches also receive special discounts and premier services through WCA's growing number of ministry partners — Select Service Providers.

For specific information about WCA membership, upcoming conferences, and other ministry services contact:

Willow Creek Association
P.O. Box 3188, Barrington, IL 60011-3188
Phone: 847-570-9812
Fax: 847-765-5046
www.willowcreek.com

NOTES

NOTES

NOTES

NOTES

NOTES

NOTES

Resources You've Been Waiting For ...

To Build the Church You've Been Dreaming About

Willow Creek Resources

What do you dream about for your church?

At the Willow Creek Association we have a dream for the church ... one that envisions the local church—your church—as the focal point for individual and community transformation.

We want to partner with you to make this happen. We believe when authentic, life-changing resources become an integral part of everyday life at your church—and when they become an extension of how your ministries function—transformation is inevitable.

It then becomes normal for people to:
- identify their personal style of evangelism and use it to bring their unchurched friends to Christ
- grow in their ability to experience God's presence with them in each moment of the day
- feel a deep sense of community with others
- discover their spiritual gifts and put them to use in ministry
- use their resources in ways that honor God and care for others

If this is the kind of church you're dreaming about, keep reading. The following pages highlight just a few of the many Willow Creek Resources available to help you. Together, we can build a local church that transforms lives and transfigures communities. We can build a church that *prevails*.

Experience the Reality of God's Presence Every Day

An Ordinary Day with Jesus

John Ortberg and Ruth Haley Barton

An Ordinary Day with Jesus uses aspects of an ordinary day and illustrates how we can connect with Jesus in those moments. Participants will learn how to:

- wake up and go to sleep in Jesus' name
- review their day with God
- silence competing voices in order to hear God's leadings
- experience time alone with God as an opportunity not an obligation
- use their own unique spiritual pathway to connect with God
- eliminate hurry and simplify their pace of life
- and much more!

Kit	0310245877
PowerPoint® CD-ROM	0310245885
Video	0310245575
Leader's Guide	0310245850
Participant's Guide	0310245869

Link People and Their Gifts with Ministries and Their Needs

Network

Bruce Bugbee, Don Cousins, Bill Hybels

This proven, easy-to-use curriculum helps participants to discover their unique spiritual gifts, areas of passion for service, and individual ministry style.

Network helps believers better understand who God made them to be, and mobilizes them into meaningful service in the local church.

Using *Network,* your whole church can share a vision for each member and understand the vital role each plays in building God's Kingdom.

Leader's Guide	0310412412
Participant's Guide	0310412315
Drama Vignettes Video	0310411890
Overhead Masters	0310485282
Consultant's Guide	0310412218
Vision/Consultant Training Video	0310244994
Implementation Guide	0310432618
Complete Kit	0310212790

Train Believers to Share Christ Naturally

Becoming a Contagious Christian

Mark Mittelberg, Lee Strobel, Bill Hybels

Over 500,000 believers have been trained to share their faith confidently and effectively with this proven curriculum. In eight, fifty-minute sessions, participants experience the joy of discovering their own unique evangelism style, learn how to transition conversations to spiritual topics, present gospel illustrations, and more.

Leader's Guide	0310500818
Participant's Guide	0310501016
Drama Vignettes Video	0310201691
Overhead Masters	0310500915
Complete Kit	0310501091

Also available—*Becoming a Contagious Christian* University Edition Video. Developed in partnership with InterVarsity Christian Fellowship, these drama vignettes feature college students building relationships with seekers. Designed to be used with the adult version of the curriculum.

Equip Students to Lead this Generation to Christ

Becoming a Contagious Christian Youth Edition

Mark Mittelberg, Lee Strobel, Bill Hybels

Revised and expanded for students by Bo Boshers

The award-winning *Becoming a Contagious Christian* curriculum has been revised and expanded to equip junior high and high school students to be contagious with their faith.

In eight, fifty-minute sessions, students learn how to:

- Develop relationships intentionally
- Transition an ordinary conversation to a spiritual conversation
- Tell their personal story of meeting Christ
- Share the gospel message using two different illustrations
- Answer ten common objections to Christianity
- Pray with a friend to receive Christ

Real stories of students who have led their friends to Christ make the material come alive as students see how God can work through them.

Leader's Guide	0310237718
Student's Guide	0310237734
Drama Vignettes Video	0310237742
Complete Kit	0310237696

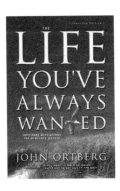

Experience Transformation in Community with Others

Pursuing Spiritual Transformation Series

John Ortberg, Laurie Pederson,
Judson Poling

Explore fresh, biblically-based ways to think about and experience life with God through Willow Creek's Five Gs: Grace, Growth, Groups, Gifts, and Good Stewardship (Giving). Each study challenges the popular notion that merely "trying harder" will lead to Christlikeness. Instead, this series helps you identify the practices, experiences, and relationships God can use to help you become the person he longs for you to be.

Fully Devoted	0310220734
Grace	0310220742
Growth	0310220750
Groups	0310220769
Gifts	0310220777
Giving	0310220785

Life-changing Small Group Resources

InterActions Series

Bill Hybels

InterActions studies encourage participants to share interests, experiences, values, and lifestyles, and uses this common ground to foster honest communication, deeper relationships, and growing intimacy with God.

Authenticity	031020674X
Community	0310206774
Lessons in Love	0310206804
Marriage	0310206758
The Real You	0310206820
Commitment	0310206839
Essential Christianity	0310224438
Evangelism	0310206782
Freedom	0310217172
Getting a Grip	0310224446
Parenthood	0310206766
Serving Lessons	0310224462
Overcoming	0310224454
Character	0310217164
Fruits of the Spirit	0310213150
Jesus	0310213169
Prayer	0310217148
Psalms	0310213185
Transparency	0310217156
Transformation	0310213177

New Community Series

Bill Hybels, John Ortberg

New Community studies provide in-depth Bible study, thought-provoking questions, and community building exercises so groups can grow in faith together.

1 John: Love Each Other	0310227682
1 Peter: Stand Strong	0310227739
Acts: Build Community	0310227704
Colossians: Discover the New You	0310227690
Exodus: Journey Toward God	0310227712
James: Live Wisely	0310227674
Philippians: Run the Race	0310233143
Romans: Find Freedom	0310227658

Walking with God Series

Don Cousins, Judson Poling

Practical, interactive, and biblically based, this dynamic series follows a two-track approach. Series 1 plugs new believers into the transforming power of discipleship to Christ. Series 2 guides mature believers into a closer look at the church.

Series 1		Series 2	
"Follow Me"	0310591635	Building Your Church	031059183X
Friendship with God	0310591430	Discovering Your Church	0310591732
The Incomparable Jesus	0310591538	Impacting Your World	0310591937
Leader's Guide	0310592038	Leader's Guide	0310592135

Tough Questions Series

Garry Poole, Judson Poling

Created for seeker small groups, this series guides participants through an exploration of key questions about and objections to Christianity.

How Does Anyone Know God Exists?	0310245028	Don't All Religions Lead to God?	0310245060
What Difference Does Jesus Make?	0310245036	Do Science and the Bible Conflict?	031024507X
How Reliable Is the Bible?	0310245044	Why Become a Christian?	0310245087
How Could God Allow Suffering/Evil?	0310245052	Leader's Guide	0310245095

Build a Church Where Nobody Stands Alone

Building a Church of Small Groups

Bill Donahue, Russ Robinson

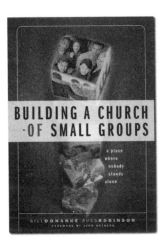

To provide the kind of authentic community people are hungry for, churches must be built on the foundation of little communities— small groups. Experience the vision, values, and necessary initial steps to begin transitioning your church from a church *with* small groups to a church *of* small groups in this groundbreaking book.

Hardcover   0310240352

The Connecting Church

Randy Frazee

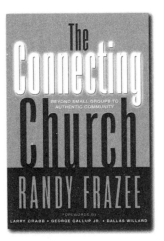

Pastor Randy Frazee explores the three essential elements of connecting churches: Common Purpose, Common Place, and Common Possessions. An excellent resource to help leaders create the kind of church where every member feels a deep sense of connection.

Hardcover   0310233089

Leading Life-Changing Small Groups

Bill Donahue

Used by thousands of leaders at Willow Creek and around the world, *Leading Life-Changing Small Groups* covers everything from starting, structuring, leading, and directing an effective small group, to developing effective leaders.

Softcover   0310247500

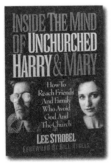
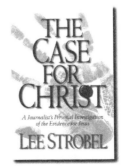

The Case for Christ Student Edition

Lee Strobel with Jane Vogel

Based on the bestselling book for adults, the student edition is a fast, fun, informative tour through the evidence for Christ designed especially for students.
Softcover   0310234840

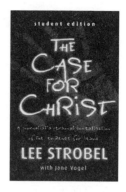

The Case for Faith

Lee Strobel

Tackles eight obstacles to faith, such as suffering, the doctrine of hell, evolution, and more.
Softcover   0310234697

The Journey

Uniquely designed to help spiritual seekers discover the relevance of Christianity.
Softcover   031092023X

Christianity 101

Gilbert Bilezikian

Explores eight core beliefs of the Christian faith. A great resource for both seekers and believers.
Softcover   0310577012

Proven Resources for Church Leaders

Rediscovering Church

Lynne and Bill Hybels

Rediscovering Church relates the beginnings of Willow Creek Community Church as well as its joys and struggles, and the philosophy and strategies behind its growth.

Softcover   0310219272